THINK BIG, WIN BIG:

Converting the Wealth in your Mind to Reality.

BY

B. O EMMA

TABLE OF CONTENTS

INTRODUCTION

Basically, everything starts with the mind. You become what you think. Do you want to live in that beautiful mansion, drive the best car, own a well-established business, and marry the most beautiful woman? It all starts with the mind. How do you make that dream, aspirations, and money in your mind become a reality?

This book will not only reveal to us extraordinary ways to make money, but it'll also teach us how to channel our minds and energy into the technical know-how of money.

CHAPTER ONE

The Option to be Rich.

Anything that might be said in recognition of destitution, the reality stays that it is preposterous to expect to carry on with a total or fruitful life except if one is rich. No man can ascend to his most prominent conceivable level in ability or soul improvement except if he has a lot of cash; for to unfurl the spirit and to foster ability he should have numerous things to utilize, and he can't have these things except if he has the means to purchase them with.

Man creates as a main priority, soul, and body by utilizing things, and society is coordinated to the point that man should have the means to turn into the holder of things; subsequently, the premise of all progression for man should be the study of getting rich. The object of all life is an improvement, and all that lives have a natural right to all the advancement it is fit for accomplishing. Man's on the right track to live imply his entitlement to have the unhindered utilization of the multitude of things that might be important to his fullest mental, profound, and actual unfoldment; or, at the end of the day, his entitlement to be rich.

In this book, I will not metaphorically discuss wealth; to be rich doesn't mean to be happy with a bit. No man should be happy with a tad on the off chance that he is fit for utilizing and getting a charge out of something else. The reason for Nature is the headway and unfoldment of life; and each man ought to have all that can add to the influence, tastefulness, excellence, and extravagance of life; to be satisfied with less is evil.

The one who possesses all he needs for the living of all the everyday routine he is equipped for experience is rich, and no man who doesn't have a lot of cash can have all he needs. Life has progressed up until this point, and become so perplexing, that even the most conventional man or lady requires a lot of abundance to live in a way that even methodologies fulfill. Each individual normally needs to turn out to be all that he is fit for turning into; this longing to acknowledge inborn conceivable outcomes is intrinsic in human instinct; we can't resist the urge to need to be everything that could be seen.

Progress in life is becoming what you need to be; you can become what you need to be excluded by utilizing things, and you can have the free utilization of things just as you become rich enough to get them. Understanding the study of getting rich is consequently the most fundamental of all information.

Nothing bad can be said about needing to get rich. The longing for wealth is the craving for a more extravagant, fuller, and more plentiful life; and that want is laudable. A man who doesn't want to live more plentifully is strange, thus a man who doesn't want to have sufficient means to purchase all he needs is unusual.

There are three thought processes in which we live; we live for the body, we live for the brain, and we live for the spirit. Nobody of these is preferable or holier over the other; all are similarly attractive, and nobody of the three — body, psyche, or soul — can live completely if both of the others are stopped of full life and articulation. There's something wrong with it or respectable to live just for the spirit and deny the psyche or body, and it is inappropriate to live for the mind and deny body and soul. We are familiar with the odious outcomes of living for the body and denying both brain and soul; and we see the genuine method of this total articulation of everything that could be given forward through body, psyche, and soul. Anything he might say, no man can be cheerful or fulfilled except if his body is living completely in each capability, opt equivalent is valid for his brain and his spirit. Any place there is an unexpressed chance, or capability not performed, there is unsatisfied longing. Want is plausible looking for articulation or capability looking for execution. Man can't live completely in that frame of mind without great food, open fire, and the war the m sanctuary; and without independence from over-the-top work. Rest and diversion are additionally important to his genuine life. He can't live completely as a top priority without books and time to concentrate on them, without a potential open door for movement and perception, or without scholarly friendship.

To live completely as a primary concern he should have scholarly diversions and should encircle himself with every one of the objects of craftsmanship and magnificence he is equipped for utilizing and appreciating. To live completely in the spirit, man should have endlessly love is denied articulation by neediness. Man's most noteworthy bliss is found in the bestowal of advantages on those he cherishes; love tracks down its most normal and unconstrained articulation in giving. The one who doesn't have anything to give can't fill his place as a spouse or father, as a resident, or as a man. In the utilization of material things man tracks down full life for his body, fosters his psyche, and unfurls his spirit. It is thusly of preeminent significance to him that he ought to be rich. It is entirely correct that you ought to want to be rich; if you are a typical man or lady, you can't resist the urge to do as such. It is completely correct that you ought to concentrate on the Study of Getting Rich, for it is the noblest and generally vital of all reviews. If you disregard this review, you are neglected in your obligation to yourself, to God, and to mankind; for you can deliver God and humankind no more prominent help than to take full advantage of yourself.

CHAPTER TWO

There is a Study on Getting Rich.

There is a Study of getting rich, and it is a precise science, similar to variable-based math or number juggling. Certain regulations oversee securing wealth; when these regulations are learned and complied with by any man, he will get rich with numerical sureness.

The responsibility for any property comes because of getting things done with a particular goal in mind; the people who get things done in this Specific Manner, whether deliberately or unintentionally, get rich; while the people who don't get things done in this Specific Manner, regardless of how hard they work or how capable they are, stay poor. A characteristic regulation like causes generally produce like results; and, thusly, any man or lady who figures out how to get things done in this Specific Manner will faultlessly get rich.

That the above assertion is valid is shown by the accompanying realities: — Getting rich doesn't involve climate, for, assuming that it was, all individuals in specific areas would become well off; individuals of one city would be generally rich, while those of different towns would be generally poor; or the occupants of one state would move in abundance, while those of an abutting state would be in destitution.

Yet, wherever we see rich and unfortunate residing next to each other, in a similar climate, and frequently participating in similar jobs. At the point when two men are in a similar region, and a similar business and one gets rich while the other remaining parts are poor, it shows that getting rich isn't, principally, an issue of climate. A few circumstances might be extra objective than others, nonetheless when two men in a related business are in a similar region, and one gets rich while the other fizzles, it demonstrates that getting rich is the consequence of getting things done with a particular goal in mind.

Also, further, the capacity to get things done in this Specific Manner isn't expected exclusively to the ownership of ability, for some individuals who have extraordinary ability stay poor, while other people who have almost no ability get rich.

Concentrating on individuals who have rich, we observe that they are a typical part in all regards, having no more prominent gifts and capacities than different men. They don't get rich since they have gifts and capacities that different men don't, but they end up getting things done with a particular goal in mind.

Getting rich isn't the aftereffect of saving, or "frugality"; numerous extremely penurious individuals are poor, while free spenders frequently get rich. Nor is getting rich due to doing things that others neglect to do; for two men in a similar business frequently do practically the same things, and one gets rich while the other remaining parts are poor or become bankrupt. From everything, we should reason that getting rich is the consequence of getting things done with a specific goal in mind. Assuming that getting rich is the consequence of getting things done with a specific goal in mind, and if like causes generally produce like outcomes, any man or lady who can get things done in that manner can become rich, and the entire matter is brought inside the space of definite science.

The inquiry emerges here, whether this Specific Way may not be challenging to such an extent that a couple might follow it. This can't be valid, as we have seen, undoubtedly. Gifted individuals get rich, and numbskulls get rich; mentally splendid individuals get rich, and exceptionally boneheads get rich; resilient individuals get rich, and feeble and wiped out individuals get rich.

A level of capacity to think and comprehend is, obviously, fundamental; however, to the extent that inherent capacity is concerned, any man or lady who has sufficient sense to peruse and comprehend these words can positively get rich. Likewise, we have seen that it's anything but an issue of the climate. Area means something; one wouldn't go to the core of the Sahara and hope to do effective business.

Getting rich includes the need of managing men, and of being where there are individuals to manage, and if these individuals are leaned to bargain in the manner you need to bargain, that would be preferable. However, that is probably the extent to which the climate goes. If any other person in your town can get rich, so can you; and if any other person in your state can get rich, so can you.

Once more, it's anything but a question of picking some specific business or calling. Individuals get wealthy in each business, and each calling; while their nearby neighbors with a similar livelihood stay in need. You will be sure best in a business that you like, and which is friendly to you, and assuming you have specific gifts which are advanced, you will truly do best in a business that requires the activity of those gifts. Likewise, you will truly do best in a business that is fit to your territory; a frozen yogurt parlor would improve in a warm environment than in Greenland.

Be that as it may, besides these overall restrictions, getting rich isn't subject to your participating in some specific business, yet upon your figuring out how to get things done with a particular goal in mind. Assuming you are presently in business, and any other person in your territory is getting wealthy in a similar business, while you are not getting rich, it is because you are not getting things done similarly that the other individual is doing them.

Nobody is kept from getting rich by the absence of capital. Valid, as you get capital the increment becomes simpler and faster; yet one who has capital is now rich, and doesn't have to consider how to turn out to be so. Regardless of how unfortunate you might be, on the off chance that you start to get things done with a particular goal in mind, you will start to get rich; and you will start to have capital. Getting ital is a piece of the most common way of getting rich, and it is a piece of the outcome that constantly follows the doing of things with a particular goal in mind.

You might be the most unfortunate man on the mainland, and be profoundly underwater; you might have neither one of the companions, impact nr assets; however assuming you start to get things done along these lines, you should dependably start to get rich, for like causes should create like outcomes. Assuming you have no capital, you can get capital; on the off chance that you are in some unacceptable business, you can get into the right business; assuming you are in some unacceptable area, you can go to the right area; and you can do as such by starting in your current business and in your current area to get things done in the Specific Manner which causes achievement.

CHAPTER THREE

Is Opportunity Cornered?

No man is kept poor since the opportunity has been detracted from him; because others have consumed the riches, and have put a wall around it. You might be separated from taking part in business in specific lines, yet there are different channels open to you. Presumably, it would be difficult for you to oversee any of the extraordinary railroad frameworks; that field is truly cornered. In any case, the electric railroad business is still in its early stages and offers a lot of extension for big business, and it will be nevertheless not many years until traffic and transportation through the air will turn into an extraordinary industry, and every one of its branches will give work to many thousands, and maybe to millions, of individuals. Why not direct your concentration toward the advancement of elevated transportation, rather than rivaling J. J. Slope and others for an opportunity in the steam rail route world?

It is, all in all, a fact that assuming you are a laborer in the utilize of the steel trust you have next to no possibility of turning into the proprietor of the plant in which you work; yet it is likewise a fact that assuming that you will start acting with a specific goal in mind, you can before long leave the utilize of the steel trust; you can purchase a ranch of from ten to forty sections of land, and take part in business as a maker of staples. There is an incredible open door as of now for men who will live upon little lots of land and develop the equivalent seriously; such men will surely get rich. You might say that you can't get the land, yet I will demonstrate to you that it isn't unimaginable and that you can unquestionably get a homestead assuming that you will go to work with a particular goal in mind.

At various periods the tide of change sets this way and that, as indicated by the requirements of the Entire, and the specific phase of social advancement which has been reached. As of now, America, it is setting toward agribusiness and unified enterprises and callings. Today, the open door is open before the rancher in his line more than before the assembly line laborer in his line. Open before the financial specialist supplies the rancher more than before the person who supplies the assembly line laborer;

and before the expert man who holds up upon the rancher more than before the person who serves the average workers.

Opportunity is plentiful for the one who will go with the tide, rather than attempt to swim against it. So the assembly line laborers, either as people or as a class, are not denied of chance. The laborers are not being "held down" by their lords; they are not being "ground" by the trusts and mixes of capital. As a class, they are where they are because they don't get things done with a particular goal in mind. If the specialists of America decided to do such, they could follow the case of their siblings in Belgium and different nations, and layout extraordinary retail chains and helpful enterprises; they could choose men of their group for office, and pass regulations leaning toward the improvement of such co-employable ventures, and in a couple of years they could take tranquil ownership of the modern field.

The middle class might turn into the expert class at whatever point they start to get things done with a specific goal in mind; the law of abundance is an ideal same for them for what it's worth for all others. This they should learn, and they will remain where they are as long as they keep on doing as they do. The singular specialist, be that as it may, isn't held somewhere around the obliviousness or the psychological lethargy of his group; he can follow the tide of the chance to wealth, and this book will let him know how.

Nobody is kept in neediness by shortness] in the stock of wealth; there is all that could be needed for all. A royal residence as extensive as the legislative center at Washington may be worked for each family on earth from the structure material in the US alone; and under escalated development, this nation would deliver fleece, cotton, material, and silk enough to dress every individual on the planet better than Solomon was shown in the entirety of his greatness; along with food enough to lavishly take care of all. The noticeable inventory is essentially limitless, and the imperceptible stock IS unlimited. All that you see on earth is produced using one unique substance, out of which all things continue.

New structures are continually being made, and more seasoned ones are dissolving, however, all are shapes expected by A certain something. There is no restriction to the stock of Nebulous Stuff or Unique Substance. The universe is made from it, yet it was not all utilized in making the universe. The spaces in, through, and between the types of the noticeable universe are saturated and loaded up with the First Substance; with the Nebulous Stuff; with the unrefined substance, all things considered. 10,000 fold the amount of as has been made could, in any case, be made, and, surprisingly, then, at that point, we shouldn't have depleted the stockpile of general natural substance.

No man, along these lines, is poor since nature is poor, or because it isn't sufficient to go around. Nature is a boundless storage facility of wealth; the inventory won't ever run low. Unique Substance is buzzing with inventive energy and is continually delivering more structures. At the point when the stock of building material is depleted, more will be delivered; when the dirt is depleted with the goal that groceries and materials for apparel will never again develop upon it, it will be restored or more soil will be made. At the point when all the gold and silver have been dug from the earth, on the off chance that a man is still in such a phase of social improvement that he wants gold and silver, more will be created from the Nebulous. The Indistinct Stuff answers the necessities of man; it won't leave him alone with no beneficial thing. This is valid for man by and large; the race, in general, is in every case bounteously rich, and assuming people are poor, it is because following the Specific Approach to doing things that makes the singular man rich.

The Shapeless Stuff is wise; stuff thinks. It is alive and is constantly induced toward more life. It is the normal and innate motivation of life to try to live more; it is the idea of insight to expand itself, and of awareness to look to broaden its limits and track down more full articulation. The universe of structures has been made by Indistinct Living Substance, hurling itself entirely into the structure to completely put itself out there more. The universe is an incredible Living Presence, continuously moving innately toward additional life and fuller working. Nature is shaped for the headway of life; its prompting thought process is the increment of life. For this purpose, all that which can pastor to live is abundantly given; there can be no need except if

God is to go against himself and invalidate his works. You are not kept poor by need the stock of wealth; it is a reality which I will exhibit a little farther on that even the assets of the Shapeless Stockpile are at the order of the man or lady who will act and think with a particular goal in mind.

CHAPTER FOUR

The Primary Standard in the Study of Getting Rich.

Believed is the main influence that can deliver substantial wealth from the Undefined Substance. The stuff from which everything is made is a substance that thinks, and an idea of structure in this substance creates the structure. Unique Substance moves as per its contemplations; each structure and cycle you find in nature is the noticeable articulation of an idea in Unique Substance. As the Indistinct Stuff thinks about a structure, it takes that structure; as it thinks about a movement, it makes that movement. That is the way all things were made. We live in an ideal world, which is essential for an idea universe.

The possibility of a moving universe stretched out all through Shapeless Substance, and the Reasoning Stuff moving as indicated by that suspect, appeared as frameworks of planets and keeps up with that structure. Thinking Substance appears as its naturally suspected, and moves as per the naturally suspected. Holding the possibility of a surrounding arrangement of suns and universes, it appears as these bodies and moves them as it suspects. Thinking about the type of a sluggish developing oak tree, it moves in like manner and produces the tree, however, hundreds of years might be expected to accomplish the work. In making, the Nebulous appears to move as per the lines of movement it has laid out; the prospect of an oak tree doesn't cause the moment development of a completely mature tree, yet it begins moving the powers which will deliver the tree, along laid out lines of development.

Each considered structure, held in thinking Substance, causes the making of the structure, yet consistently, or possibly for the most part, along lines of development and activity previously settled. The prospect of a place of a specific development, if it were presented for Shapeless Substance, probably won't cause the moment development of the house; however, it would cause the turning of imaginative energies previously working in exchange and trade into such directs as to bring about the expedient structure of the house. Furthermore, assuming there were no current channels through which the imaginative energy could work, then, at that point, the house would be shaped straightforwardly from the basic substance, without sitting tight to the sluggish cycles of the natural and inorganic world. No considered structure can be put forth for Unique Substance without causing the making of the structure. Man is a reasoning community, and can begin with a thought. Every one of the structures that man styles with his hands should first exist in quite a while though; he can't shape a thing until he has believed that thing.

Thus far man has restricted his endeavors completely to crafted by his hands; he has applied difficult work to the universe of structures, looking to change or adjust those generally existing. He has never considered attempting to cause the making of new structures by putting forth his contemplations for Amorphous Substance.

At the point when a man has a thought structure, he takes material from the types of nature and makes a picture of the structure which is to him. He has, up to this point, put forth practically zero attempts to co-work with Undefined Knowledge;

to work "with the Dad." He has not envisioned that he can "do what he seeth the Dad doing." Man reshapes and changes existing structures by physical work; he has focused on whether or not he may not deliver things from Shapeless Substance by imparting his considerations to it. We propose to demonstrate that he might do as such; to demonstrate that any man or lady might do as such, and to show how. As our initial step, we should set down three major recommendations.

To begin with, we declare that there is one unique amorphous stuff, or substance, from which everything is made. Every one of the numerous components is nevertheless various introductions of one component; every one of the many structures found in natural and inorganic nature is nevertheless various shapes, produced using similar stuff. Furthermore, this stuff is thinking stuff; an idea held in it creates the type of the idea. Thought, in thinking substance, produces shapes. Man is a reasoning place, fit for the unique idea; if a man can convey his thinking to a unique reasoning substance, he can cause the creation, or development, of what he thinks about. To sum up this: — There is reasoning stuff from which everything is made, and which, in its unique state, pervades, enters, and fills the interspaces of the universe.

An idea, in this substance, creates what is imaged by the idea. Man can frame things in his idea, and, by presenting his thinking for shapeless substance, can cause what he thinks going to be made. It very well might be inquired as to whether I can demonstrate these assertions; and without delving into subtleties, I answer that I can do as such, both by rationale and experience.

Thinking back on the peculiarities of structure and thought, I come to one unique reasoning substance; and thinking forward from this thinking substance, I come to labor supply to cause the arrangement of what he thinks about. Also, by trying to view as the thinking valid; and this is my most grounded verification.

Assuming small time who peruses this book gets rich by doing everything that it says to him to do, that is proof on the side of my case; however assuming each man who does everything it says to him to do gets rich, which is positive confirmation until somebody goes through the interaction and comes up short. The hypothesis is valid until the cycle falls flat; and this interaction won't come up short, for each man who does precisely the exact thing this book advises him to do will get rich. I have said that men get rich by getting things done with a specific goal in mind; and to do as such, men should become ready to think with a specific goal in mind.

A man's approach to doing things is the immediate consequence of how he ponders things. To get things done in the manner you believe should do them, you should obtain the capacity to think how you need to think; this is the most important move toward getting rich. To think what you need to believe is to think TRUTH, paying little mind to appearances. Each man has the regular and innate ability to think what he needs to think, however, it expects more work to do as such than it does to think] the considerations which are proposed by appearances.

To think as per appearances is simple; to think truth paying little heed to appearances is difficult, and requires the use of more power than some other work man is called upon to perform. There is no work from which the vast majority recoil as they do from that of maintained and back-to-back thought; it is the hardest work on the planet. Each appearance in the noticeable world will in general deliver a relating structure in the brain which notices it, and this must be forestalled by holding the possibility of Reality.

To view the presence of sickness will create the type of the illness in your brain, and eventually in your body, except if you hold the prospect of reality, which is that there is no sickness; it is just an appearance and acting. To view the appearances of destitution will create comparing structures in your brain except if you hold to the reality that there is no neediness; there is just overflow.

To think wellbeing when encircled by the appearances of infection, or to think wealth when in appearances of destitution, requires influence; however, he who secures this influence turns into a Brains. He can vanquish destiny; he can have what he needs. This power must be gained by getting hold of the fundamental truth that is behind all appearances; and that reality is that there is one Reasoning Substance, from which and by which everything is made. Then we should understand the reality that each thought held in this substance turns into a structure, and that man can so put forth his considerations for It as to make them take structure and become noticeable things.

At the point when we understand this, we lose all uncertainty and dread, for we realize that we can make what we need to make; we can get what we need to have, and can become what we need to be. As an initial move toward getting rich, you should accept the three essential assertions given beforehand in this section; and to underscore them, I rehash them here: —

There is reasoning stuff from which everything is made, and which, in its unique state, pervades, enters, and fills the interspaces of the universe. An idea, in this substance, creates what is imaged by the idea. Man can shape things in his idea, and, by putting forth his thinking for undefined substance, can cause what he thinks going to be made.

You should dismiss any remaining ideas of the universe than this monistic one, and you should stay upon this until it is fixed to you, and has turned into your constant thought. Peruse these doctrine explanations over once more; fix each word upon your memory, and think upon them until you solidly accept what they say. On the off chance that uncertainty comes to you, cast it to the side as wrongdoing. Try not to pay attention to contentions against this thought; don't go to chapels or talks where an opposite idea of things is educated or taught. Try not to understand magazines or books which show an alternate thought; on the off chance that you get stirred up in your confidence, every one of your endeavors will be to no end. Try not to inquire as to why these things are valid, nor hypothesize regarding how they can be valid; just accept them based on previous experience. The study of getting rich starts with the outright acknowledgment of this confidence.

CHAPTER FIVE

Expanding Life.

You should dispose of the last remnant of the old thought that there is a Divinity whose will it is that you ought to be poor, or whose reasons might be served by keeping you in neediness. The Canny Substance which is All, and on the whole, and which daily routines take all things together and lives in you, is a deliberately Living Substance. Being an intentionally living substance, It should have the regular and inborn craving of every living knowledge to increment life. Each living thing must constantly look for the broadening of its life, since life, in the simple demonstration of living, should expand itself.

A seed dropped into the ground, springs into movement, and in the demonstration of living produces 100 additional seeds; life, by living, duplicates itself. It is perpetually turning out to be more; it should do so on the off chance that it keeps on being by any means. Insight is under this equivalent need for ceaseless increment. Each thought we figure makes it essential for us to think one more thought; awareness is consistently extending. Each reality we learn drives us to the learning of another reality; information is persistently expanding. Each ability we develop brings to the brain the longing to develop another ability; we are dependent upon the inclination of life, looking for articulation, which overdrives us on to know more, accomplish more, and be more.

To know more, accomplish more, and be more we should have; we should have things to use, for we learn, and do, and become, simply by utilizing things. We should get rich with the goal that we can live more. The craving for wealth is concerning bigger life looking for satisfaction; each want is the work of an unexpressed chance to come right into it. It is power looking to show which causes want. That which gets you to need more cash flow is equivalent to that which makes the plant develop; it is Life, looking for more full articulation.

The One Living Substance should be dependent upon this innate law of all life; it is saturated with the craving to live more; for that reason, it is under the need of making things. The One Substance wants to live more in you;

subsequently, it maintains that you should have everything you can utilize.

God wants that you ought to get rich. He believes that you should get rich since he can articulate his thoughts better through you assuming you have a lot of things to use in giving him articulation. He can live more in you assuming that you have limitless order of the method for life. The universe wants you to have all that you need to have. Nature is well disposed to your arrangements. Everything is normal for you. Decide that this is valid.

It is fundamental, notwithstanding, that your motivation ought to blend with the reason that is altogether. You should need reality, not simple delight or arousing satisfaction. Life is the presentation of capability; and the singular lives just when he carries out each role, physical, mental, and otherworldly, of which he is skilled, without abundance in any. You would rather not get rich tonishly, for the satisfaction of creature wants; that isn't life. Yet, the presentation of every actual capability is a piece of life, and nobody lives totally who keeps the driving forces from getting the body a typical and restorative articulation. You would rather not get rich exclusively to appreciate mental joys, to get information, to delight desire, to surpass others, to be popular. Every one of these is a real piece of life, however, the man who lives for the joys of the keenness alone will just have a half-life and he won't ever be happy with his part.

You would rather not get rich exclusively to bring about some benefit for other people, to lose yourself for the salvation of humanity, to encounter the delights of magnanimity and penance. The delights of the spirit are just a piece of life, and the, and no preferred or nobler over some other part.

You need to get rich so you might eat, drink, and be cheerful when the time has come to do these things; so you might encircle yourself with delightful things, see far-off lands, feed your brain, and foster your keenness; so that adoration men and do kind things, and have the option to have a decent impact in assisting the world with tracking down reality. Yet, recollect that outrageous philanthropy is no more excellent and no nobler than outrageous childishness; both are botches.

Dispose of God's desired thought you to forfeit yourself for other people, and that you can get his approval thusly; God doesn't require anything of the sort. What he needs is that you ought to capitalize on yourself, as far as you might be concerned, and others; and you can help other people more by taking advantage of yourself than in differently. You can capitalize on yourself exclusively by getting rich; so it is correct and laudable that you ought to give you're first and best thought to craft by gaining abundance.

Keep in mind, in any case, that the craving for Substance is for all, and its development should be for more life to all; it can't be made to work for less life to any, because it is similarly, on the whole, looking for wealth and life. Shrewd Substance will make things for you, however, it won't remove things from another person and give them to you.

You should dispose of the possibility of a contest. You are to make, not to go after what is as of now made.

You don't need to remove anything from anybody.

You don't need to drive sharp deals.

You don't need to cheat or make use. You don't have to allow any man to work for you for short of what he procures.

You don't need to desire the property of others, or to take a gander at it with unrealistic eyes; no man has anything of which you can't have the like, and that without removing what he has from him. You are to turn into a maker, not a contender; you will get what you need, yet so that when you get it every other man will have more than he has now.

I'm mindful that there are men who get a huge measure of cash by continuing contrary to the assertions in the section above and may add an expression of clarification here. Men of the plutocratic kind, who become extremely rich, do so some of the time absolutely by their phenomenal capacity on the plane of rivalry; and in some cases, they unknowingly relate themselves to Substance in its extraordinary purposes and developments for the overall racial up-building through modern advancement. Rockefeller, Carnegie, Morgan, et al., have been the oblivious specialists of the Preeminent in the important work of arranging and coordinating useful industry; and eventually, their work will contribute tremendously toward expanded life for all. Their day is almost finished; they have coordinated creation, and will before long be prevailed by the specialists of the huge number, who will arrange the apparatus of appropriation.

The multi-tycoons resemble the beast reptiles of ancient times; they have a vital impact in the transformative cycle, yet similar Power which created them will discard them. Furthermore, it is well to remember that they have never been truly rich; a record of the confidential existence of a large portion of this class will show that they have been the most miserable and pathetic of poor people.

Wealth got on the serious plane is rarely agreeable and extremely durable; they are yours today, and another's tomorrow. Keep in mind, on the off chance that you are to become wealthy in a logical and certain manner, you should rise completely out of the cutthroat idea. You should never think briefly that the stockpile is restricted. Right, when you start to feel that all the cash is being "cornered" and constrained by brokers and others and that you should strive to get regulations passed to stop this interaction, etc. at that point, you drop into the serious psyche, and your ability to cause creation is away for the present; and what is more terrible, you will likely capture the innovative developments you have previously initiated.

Realize that there is an endless large number of dollars' worth of gold in the mountains of the earth, not yet uncovered; and know that on the off chance that there were not, more would be made from Figuring Substance to supply your requirements. Realize that the cash you want will come, regardless of whether 1,000 men must beery of new mother lodes tomorrow. Never take a gander at the noticeable stock; take a gander at the boundless wealth in Nebulous Substance, and realize that they are coming to you as quick as you can get and utilize them. No one, by cornering the apparent stock, can keep you from getting what is yours.

So never permit yourself to think for a moment that the very best structure spots will be taken before you prepare to fabricate your home except if you rush. Never stress over the trusts and joins, and get restless for dread they will before long come to claim the entire earth. Never get apprehensive that you will lose what you need since another individual "outsmarts you." That couldn't realistically occur; you are not looking for whatever is moved by any other person; you are causing what you need to be made from Nebulous Substance, and the inventory is unbounded. Adhere to the figured-out assertion: — there is reasoning stuff from which everything is made, and which, in its unique state, saturates, enters, and fills the interspaces of the universe.

An idea, in this substance, delivers what is imaged by the idea. Man can shape things in his idea, and, by putting forth his thinking for amorphous substance, can cause what he thinks going to be made.

CHAPTER SIX

How Wealth Come to You.

At the point when I say that you don't need to drive sharp deals, I don't imply that you need to drive no deals by any means, or that you are over the need for having any dealings with your kindred men. I imply that you won't have to manage them unreasonably; you need to get something for little more than, can provide for each man more than you take from him.

You can't give each man more in real money market esteem than you take from him, however, you can give him more being used worth than the money worth of what you take from him. The paper, ink, and other material in this book may not merit the cash you paid for it; however, if the thoughts recommended by it bring you a large number of dollars, you have not been violated by the people who offered it to you; they have given you an extraordinary use an incentive for a little money esteem.

Allow us to assume that I own an image by one of the extraordinary craftsmen, which, in any socialized local area, is worth a huge number of dollars. I take it to the Baffin Straight, and by "persuasiveness" prompt an Eskimo to give a heap of furs worth $500 for it. I have violated him, for he does not need the image; it has no utilization worth to him; it won't add to his life.

In any case, assume I give him a weapon worth $50 for his furs; then he has made a decent deal. He needs the weapon; it will get him a lot more furs and much food; it will add to his life all around; it will make him rich. At the point when you ascend from the serious to the imaginative plane, you can filter your deals stringently, and assuming that you are selling any man anything which doesn't add more to his life than what he gives you in return, you can bear to stop it. You don't need to beat anyone in the business. Furthermore, assuming you are in a business that beats individuals, receive in return without a moment's delay.

Give each man more being used worth than you take from him in real money esteem; then you are adding to the existence of the world by each deal. Assuming you have individuals working for you, you should take from them more in real money esteem than you pay them in compensation; yet you can coordinate your business so it will be loaded up with the guideline of progression, thus that every representative who wishes to do so may propel a little consistently.

You can cause your business to accomplish for your representatives how this book is doing you. You can lead your business with the goal that it will be a kind of stepping stool, by which each worker who will take the difficulty might move to wealth himself; and offered the chance on the off chance that he won't do so it isn't your issue.

Lastly, because you are to cause the production of your wealth from Undefined Substance which saturates all your current circumstances, it doesn't follow that they are to come to fruition from the environment and appear before your eyes. Assuming you need a sewing machine, for example, I don't intend to let you know that you are to dazzle the prospect of a sewing machine on Thinking Substance until the machine is framed without hands, in the room where you sit, or somewhere else. Yet, assuming that you need a sewing machine, hold the psychological picture of it with the best conviction that it is being made, or is headed to you. After once framing the idea, have the most outright and unquestioning confidence that the sewing machine is coming; never think about it, or discuss it, in some other way than as being certain to show up. Guarantee it as currently yours.

It will be brought to you by the force of the Incomparable Insight, following up on the personalities of men. If you live in Maine, a man may be brought from Texas or Japan to participate in some exchange which will bring about you getting what you need. Assuming this is the case, the entire matter will be as a lot to that man's benefit for what it's worth to yours.

Remember briefly that the Reasoning Substance is through all, altogether, speaking with all, and can impact all. The craving for Reasoning Substance for a more full life and better living has caused the making of all the sewing machines previously made; and it can cause the production of millions more, and will, at whatever point men put it into high gear by want and confidence, and by acting with a specific goal in mind. You can unquestionably have a sewing machine in your home, and it is similarly as sure that you can have some other thing or things that you need, and which you will use for the headway of your own life and the existence of others. You want not to hold back about asking generally; "it is your Dad's pleasure to give you the realm," said Jesus.

Unique Substance needs to experience all that is conceivable in you and believes you should have everything you can or will use for the living of the most bountiful life.

Assuming you fix upon your cognizance of the way that the longing you feel for the ownership of wealth is unified with the craving for Power for more complete articulation, your confidence becomes invulnerable. When I saw a young man sitting at a piano, and pointlessly attempting to free concordance once again from the keys, I saw that he was lamented and incited by his failure to play genuine music. I requested him the reason for his vexation, and he replied, "I can feel the music in me, however, I can't make my hands go right." The music in him was the Desire of Unique Substance, containing every one of the conceivable outcomes of all life; all that there is of music was looking for articulation through the youngster.

God, the One Substance, is attempting to live and do and appreciate things through humankind. He is saying, "I believe hands should fabricate magnificent designs, to play divine harmonies, to lay out wonderful pictures; I maintain that feet should get my things done, eyes to see my delights, tongues to tell powerful bits of insight, and to sing grand tunes, etc. All that there is of probability is looking for articulation through men. God needs the individuals who can play music to have pianos and every other instrument, and to possess the ability to develop their gifts to the furthest reaches; He needs the people who can see the value in excellence to have the option to encircle themselves with wonderful things; He needs the individuals who can perceive truth to have each an open door to travel and notice; He needs the individuals who can see the value in dress to be delightfully dressed and the individuals who can see the value in great food to be richly taken care of. He needs everything since Himself appreciates and values them; God needs to play, sing, partake in the magnificence, broadcast truth, wear fine garments, and eat great food sources.

"It is God that worketh in you to will and to do," said Paul.

The craving you feel for wealth is the Boundless, trying to articulate his thoughts in you as He looked to track down articulation in the young man at the piano. So you want not to hold back to generally inquire. Your part is to center and communicate the cravings of God.

This is a troublesome point with the vast majority; they hold something of the old thought that neediness and benevolence are satisfying to God. They view neediness as a piece of the arrangement, a need of nature. They have the possibility that God has completed His work and made everything that could be made, and that most men should remain poor since it isn't sufficient to go around. They hold to such a great deal of this incorrect idea that they feel embarrassed to request riches; they do whatever it takes not to need more than an exceptionally humble capability, barely enough to make them genuinely agreeable.

I review now the instance of one understudy who was informed that he should get at the top of the priority list a reasonable image of the things he wanted so his innovative idea of them may be dazzled on Shapeless Substance. He was an extremely unfortunate man, residing in a leased house, and having just what he procured from one day to another; and he was unable to embrace the way that all abundance was his. In this way, in the wake of reasoning the matter over, he concluded that he could sensibly request another mat for the floor of his best room, and an anthracite coal oven to warm the house during the chilly climate. Adhering to the guidelines given in this book, he got these things in a couple of months; and afterward, it unfolded upon him that he had not asked enough. He went through the house in which he resided and arranged every one of the upgrades he might want to make; he intellectually added a cove window here and a room there, until it was finished to him as his optimal home; and afterward, he arranged its decorations.

Holding the entire picture to him, he started residing in the Specific Way, and pushing toward what he needed; and he possesses the house now, and is remaking it after the type of his psychological picture. Furthermore, presently, with still bigger confidence, he is proceeding to get more prominent things. It has been unto him as per his confidence, and it is so with you and with us all.

CHAPTER SEVEN

Appreciation.

The outlines given in the last part will have passed on to the peruser the way that the most vital move toward finding out about your needs to the Shapeless Substance. This is valid, and you will see that to do so it becomes important to relate yourself to the Shapeless Knowledge in an agreeable manner.

To get this amicable connection involves such essential and crucial significance that I will give space to its conversation here, and give you directions which, assuming that you will follow them, will be sure to bring you into ideal solidarity of psyche with God.

The entire course of mental adjustment and penance can be summarized in a single word, appreciation. In the first place, you accept that there is one Canny Substance, from which all things continue; second, you accept that this Substance gives you all that you want; and third, you relate yourself to it by a sensation of significant appreciation.

Many individuals who request their lives properly in any remaining ways are kept in neediness by their absence of appreciation. Having gotten one gift from God, they cut the wires which interface them with Him by neglecting to makanan e affirmation.

It is straightforward that the closer we live to the wellspring of riches, the more abundance we will get; and it is simple likewise to comprehend that the spirit that is dependably appreciative lives in nearer contact with God than the one which never shifts focus over to Him in grateful affirmation. The more appreciatively we fix our brains on the Preeminent when beneficial things come to us, the more beneficial things we will get, and the more quickly they will come; the explanation essentially is that the psychological disposition of appreciation brings the brain into nearer contact with the source from which the endowments come.

If it is a groundbreaking insight to you that appreciation brings your entire brain into nearer congruity with the imaginative energies of the universe, think of it as well, and you will see that it is valid. The beneficial things you as of now have come to you along the line of dutifulness to specific regulations. Appreciation will lead your psyche out along the ways by which things come, and it will keep you together as one with an inventive idea and keep you from falling into a serious idea.

Appreciation alone can keep you looking toward the All, and keep you from falling into the blunder of reasoning of the stockpile as restricted, and to do that would be deadly to your expectations.

There is a Law of Appreciation, and you should notice the law if you are to obtain the outcomes you look for. The law of appreciation is a characteristic rule that activity and response are generally equivalent and in inverse bearings. The thankful exceeding of your psyche in grateful recognition to the Preeminent is freedom or consumption of power; it can't neglect to arrive at that to which it is tended to, and the response is an immediate development toward you.

Furthermore, if your appreciation is solid and steady, the response in Undefined Substance will areas of strength be nonstop; the development of the things you need will be consistent toward you. Notice the appreciative demeanor that Jesus took; how He generally is by all accounts saying, "I say thanks to You, Father, that Thou hearest me." You can't practice a lot of force without appreciation; for appreciation keeps you associated with Power. Yet, the worth of appreciation doesn't comprise exclusively in getting you more endowments later on. Without appreciation, you can't long keep from disappointing contemplations viewing things as they are.

The second you license your psyche to stay with disappointment upon things as they are, you start to lose ground. You fix consideration upon the normal, the customary, poor people, and the foul and mean; and your brain appears as these things. Then, at that point, you will communicate these structures or mental pictures to the Undefined, the normal, poor people, the filthy, and the mean will come to you.

To allow your brain to abide upon the sub-par is to become second-rate and to encircle yourself with mediocre things. Then again, to concentrate on the best is to encircle yourself with the best, and become the best.

The Innovative Power inside us makes us into the picture of that to which we offer our consideration. We are Thinking Substance, and thinking substance generally appears as that which it contemplates.

The thankful psyche is continually fixed upon the best; thusly it will in general turn into the best; it takes the structure or character of the best, and will get the best.

Additionally, confidence is brought into the world of appreciation. The thankful brain constantly anticipates beneficial things, and assumption becomes confidence. The response of appreciation to one's brain produces confidence, and each cordial influx of appreciative thanksgiving increments confidence. He who has no sensation of appreciation can't long hold living confidence; and without living confidence, you can't get rich by the imaginative strategy, as we will find in the accompanying sections.

It is essential, then, at that point, to develop the propensity for being appreciative of each good thing that comes to you; and to consistently express gratefulness.

Also, because all things have added to your progression, you ought to remember everything for your appreciation. Try not to sit around idly thinking or discussing the inadequacies or wrong activities of tycoons or trust magnates. Their association with the world has created your open door; all you get comes to you as a result of them. Try not to seethe against degenerate lawmakers; on the off chance that it was not for legislators we ought to fall into rebellion, and your chance would be extraordinarily decreased.

God has worked quite a while and persistently to bring us up to where we are in industry and government, and He is going right on with His work. There isn't the least uncertainty that He will get rid of tycoons, trust magnates, skippers of industry, and legislators when they can be saved; yet meanwhile, see they are excellent. Recall that they are assisting with organizing the lines of transmission along which your wealth will come to you, and be appreciative to them all. This will carry you into agreeable relations with the positive qualities in all things, and the positive qualities in all that will advance toward you.

CHAPTER EIGHT

Thinking with a particular goal in mind.

Turn around to chapter six, and read again the narrative of the one who framed a psychological picture of his home, and you will find out about the underlying move toward getting rich. You should frame a reasonable and clear mental image of what you need; you can't send a thought except if you have it yourself.

You should have it before you can give it; and many individuals disappoint Thinking Substance since they have themselves just an obscure and foggy idea of the things they need to do, have, or become. It isn't enough that you ought to want abundance "to accomplish something useful with"; everyone has that craving.

It isn't enough that you ought to have a wish to travel, see things, live more, and so on. Everyone has those wants too. On the off chance that you planned to send a remote message to a companion, you wouldn't send the letters of the letters in order in their request, and let him build the directive for himself; nor would you take words indiscriminately from the word reference. You would send an intelligible sentence; one which implied something. At the point when you attempt to put forth your needs for Substance, recall that it should be finished by a reasonable proclamation; you should understand what you need, and be unmistakable.

You can never get rich, or begin the innovative influence right into it, by conveying unformed longings and unclear cravings. Go over your longings similarly as the man I have portrayed went over his home; see exactly what you need, and get an unmistakable mental image of it as you wish it to look when you get it.

That unmistakable mental picture you should have persistently at the top of the priority list, as the mariner has as a primary concern the port toward which he is cruising the boat; you should keep your face toward it constantly. You should know more fail to focus on it than the pilot neglects to focus on the compass.

It isn't important to take practices in that frame of mind, to separate exceptional times for petition and confirmation, nor to "go into the quietness," nor to do mysterious tricks of any sort. These things are sufficient, however, all you want is to understand what you need and to need it seriously enough with the goal that it will remain in your viewpoint. Spend however a lot of your relaxation time that you can mull over your image, yet nobody necessities to take activities to focus his psyche on a thing which he needs; it is the things you couldn't care less about which expect work to fix your consideration upon them.

Also, except if you need to get rich, with the goal that the longing is sufficiently able to hold your contemplations coordinated to the reason as the attractive shaft holds the needle of the compass, it will scarcely be advantageous for you to attempt to do the guidelines given in this book.

The strategies thus put forward are for individuals whose craving for wealth is sufficiently able to defeat mental apathy and the adoration for straightforwardness, and make them work. The more clear and unmistakable you make your image, then, and the more you abide upon it, drawing out the entirety of its superb subtleties, the more grounded your craving will be, and the more grounded your longing, the simpler it will be to hold your psyche fixed upon the image of what you need.

Something more is fundamental, in any case than just seeing the image. Assuming that that is all you do, you are just a visionary and will have practically no power for achievement. Behind your unmistakable vision should be the reason to acknowledge it; to bring it out in substantial articulation.

Also, behind this reason should be a powerful and unfaltering Confidence that the thing is as of now yours; that it is "within reach" and you have just to claim it. Live in the new house, intellectually, until it takes structure around you. In the psychological domain, enter on the double into full delight in the things you need. "At all things, ye request when ye implore, accept that ye get them, and ye will have them," said Jesus.

See the things you need as though they were very you constantly; view yourself as purchasing and utilizing them. Utilize them in your creative mind similarly as you will utilize them when they are your substantial belongings. Stay up on your psychological picture until it is clear and particular, and afterward take the Psychological

Mentality of Proprietorship toward everything in that image. Claim it, at the top of the priority list, in full confidence that it is yours. Hold to this psychological proprietorship; don't falter for a moment in the confidence that it is genuine.

Furthermore, recollect information exchanged in the first part about appreciation; be as grateful for it all the time as you hope to be the point at which it has taken structure. The one who can earnestly say thanks to God for the things which at this point he possesses just in creative mind, has genuine confidence. He will get rich; he will cause the production of all he needs.

You don't have to ask more than once for the things you need; enlightening God consistently isn't required. "Utilize not vain redundancies as the barbarian do," expressed Jesus to His understudies, "for your Dad knoweth that ye need these things before ye ask Him."

Your part is to insightfully plan your longing for the things which make for a bigger life, to get these cravings organized into an intelligent entire; and afterward to present this Entire Craving for the Nebulous Substance, which has the power and the will to bring you what you need. You don't establish this connection by rehashing a series of words; you make it by holding the vision with unwavering Reason to accomplish it, and with unflinching Confidence that you truly do achieve it.

The response to petitioning heaven isn't as indicated by your confidence while you are talking, yet as per your confidence while you are working. You can't dazzle the brain of God by having a unique day off put aside to let him know what you need, and afterward failing to remember Him during the remainder of the week. You can't intrigue Him by having exceptional hours to go into your storage room and supplicate on the off chance that you, excuse the matter from your psyche until the hour of petitioning heaven comes back once more.

Oral petitioning heaven is sufficient, and makes its difference, particularly upon yourself, in explaining your vision and reinforcing your confidence; yet it isn't your oral petitions which get you what you need. To get rich you needn't bother with a "sweet hour of supplication"; you want to "ask consistently." And by petition, I mean holding consistently to your vision, with the reason to cause its creation into the strong structure, and the confidence that you are doing as such. "Accept that ye get them."

The entire matter turns on getting, whenever you have framed your vision. At the point when you have shaped it, it is ideal to offer an oral expression, tending to the Preeminent in respectful supplication; and from that second you should, as a primary concern, get what you request. Live in the new house; wear fine garments; ride in the car; go on the excursion, and with certainty plan for more prominent excursions. Think and talk about everything you have requested regarding genuine present possession. Envision a climate, and a monetary condition precisely as you need them, and experience constantly in that fanciful climate and monetary condition. Mind, nonetheless, that you don't do this as a simple visionary and visionary; hold to the Confidence that the nonexistent is being understood, and to the Reason to acknowledge it. Recollect that it is confidence and reason in the utilization of the creative mind which have the effect between the researcher and the visionary. What's more, having realized this reality, it is here that you should become familiar with the legitimate utilization of the Will.